Poetry Rooms

JOHN MACDONALD

To Ruth Johnson Macdonald from whom it all began

POETRY ROOMS

PREFACE

"Everyone must leave something behind when he dies, my grand-father said. A child or a book or a painting or a house or a wall built or a pair of shoes made. Or a garden planted. Something your hand touched some way so your soul has somewhere to go when you die, and when people look at that tree or that flower you planted, you're there."

Ray Bradbury, Fahrenheit 451

INTRODUCTION

Every dynamic family is sustained by values, intuitions and faith, passed from generation to generation. Such gifts come in the form of biographies, letters, photo albums and even dinner conversations. Historical representations of what was believed to be relevant, honest and alluring. Poetry is a cultural heritage gift, providing the magic of metaphor to help you understand yourself.

JMM

Seanchaí Room

"I am convinced that the greatest legacy we can leave our children are happy memories: those precious moments so much like pebbles on the beach that are plucked from the white sand and placed in tiny boxes that lay undisturbed on tall shelves until one day they spill out and time repeats itself, with joy and sweet sadness, in the child now an adult."

Og Mandino

"Poetry addresses individuals in their most intimate, private, frightened and elated moments . . . because it comes closer than any other art form to addressing what cannot be said. In expressing the inexpressible, poetry remains close to the origins of language."

W.S Merwin

SAND CASTLES

Our proper world
The vision
Begins for some,
With sand castles turrets and keeps
Forged beneath a Dixie cup
The castle is safe
Popsicle sticks repel in belched fire
Bad men who rush
Within a violent surge of grey sea

Under the shade of a sand dollar canopy
The Queen of polished stone
She rules
Complexion smooth
Bright marble loving eyes
The boy King—four pronged jack
He commands
Victory on victory rings
Triumphant

Death pleads her scene
Blurred image without soul
Seaweed
But the court laughs in pearls and satin
Our children, their children
Never cry

In the sigh of tired August day
Orange sun dissolves in shadow fingers
Flood tide floods
Sticks, shells and turrets
Crumble under foam

The beach is empty

Yesterday, tomorrow and forever
Sweet eternal vision
Our proper world
Remains

We walked home secure
Innocent
Small feet into large dunes
Path of love into warm showers
Mother`s set table

Behind and beyond
Salt truth unseen when facing west
Evermore
Castle
Queen
Jack King
Alive in perfect harmony

Our immutable standard
For the way things ought to be

JMM 1954
Brigantine, N.J
Summer home

CURFEW LOVE

On the night of closed mouth kisses
We loved through cashmere
Without loving
Beneath hours of staged goodbyes
We inhaled
Young acceptance for someday
Mantled tears of gray ash

    Imagined that night
    Recalled this day

Our curfew love endures
Conceived in your light kiss
Mercifully
Never defined

                                        JMM
                                        1960

                            Teen age romance memories

8

SIX YEAR OLD BOY

There is little to do for a six year old boy
His brother is out with a friend
He plays on the floor with a small Christmas toy
And dreams of dad`s flags in the wind

The world is so big when you`r not very tall
There are so many things that can please
Asked what are you doing he says, "nothing at all"
When he`s big he`ll do nothing with ease

The secrets of youth fill all of his days
Fine gifts that innocence brings
He does so much in innumerable ways
No need for material things

In years to come he`ll long for the joy
Of the quiet days for a six year old boy

JMM
1981

SHARING THE NIGHT`S HONOR

They came through the trees
When the moon was full, when their pond
Lay beamed in ribbons
Of sparkling promise and anodynes
Bobbing in moonlight
Streams that warmed the cloudless chill

They knelt on the shore together
Toasting reflected smiles
Drinking the light from unlike cups
This a crystal whisper
That of tempered brass, discovered gold
A ladle of oak
And one from the palm of his hand

They sang in the cadence of fragile time
Filling their hearts with silver
Sharing the night`s honor
Until the water was gone
Their emotions dry and the light dissolved
In a bog of endless sand

Each man returned to his valley
A prisoner
Of schemes and expectations
Lost in a spectral wisp of ashen dreams
Stinging the eyes
With lightless despair

Softly, to the sigh of his return
She smiled
As given a thousand times before
Unfelt, until now, when the glow
From her outstretched arms
Brightened the stars
And the warmth of her light
Was all around him

JMM
1988

*Five professional friends privately sharing
monthly haute cuisine dinners*

BLACK LIGHTS

Tonight I suffer the roar of your tormentors
Strangers to your bursting heart
Tonight I prompt the spasm of the effort
To rise beneath those black lights

Fallen before the rage of unknown those
Survives the moan of a fighting man
While salt beads from God`s perspiration
Flush in the foam of ten thousand pints

Rise proudly dear son
From the cold of those black lights
Rise proudly
To the roar within you

    My blood begets your bleeding
    Your doubt tests my hope
    My mouth dries in your sweat
    Your young revives my old
    And the force of your effort proves
    The worth of my own

There can never be a stronger hope
There will never be a firmer yes
In answer to this violent game
Stand to the now that is against you
Accept my arm for just this time

Inhale the glory of your try
Protect yourself at all times
And your eyes
Bless me with a nod.

JMM
Ruddock vs. Lewis
Heavyweight Fight
Earls Court
London, England
October 1992

BEING NECESSARY

It was a morning of soft rain
On the blue water beyond the porch
The transparent wall
Protecting me
From being necessary

It feels good to do nothing
And to have nothing to show for it
An odd discipline
Staring musing forgetting
The capital of Mozambique

My mind floats
Beyond those drifting bits
My father's hands
The pigtailed friend in fifth grade
A fleeting moment of regret

Summer days warm you
With indulgent ease
A lovely aimlessness
Like a novel never finished
Timeless time escaping
            Being necessary

JMM
Duck Key-2018

THE PATH

Passover and Easter
Embolden by the message
Driven by the truth
Effective wound care
For the poorest of the poor
      Somehow
      Somehow
We must find the path

JMM
2019

POETRY ROOMS

I treasure drifting hours of being
When memories weave thru poems
Birthed in former days
That spoke to my condition

A picture is worth a thousand words
A poem a million dreams
Revealed by a hidden light switch accessible
Only to you while reading yourself

Each room is to its own
Pressing an ear to a son`s Christmas joy
Recalling old friends
By their response to my words

May I come in and sit with you a while
Allow me to again taste
Your tears discovered in the last line
Within the quiet of the night

How effortless to walk across oceans
Into nightmares devoid the abundance of life
Feeling the moans and drumbeats that question
Any workable arrangement with God

Every poetry room offers two faces
One for the reader one for the poet
Past time - own time - eternity time
Each raising the curtain on who we are

JMM
2020

Christmas Room

*"Life without a shared ritual and some kind of
sacred myth is hardly worth living."*
C.S. Lewis

*"Why the transcendent? What a child's belief in
Christmas gives to the joy of life."*
Anon.

AFTER FIFTEEN YEARS

After fifteen years there is a feeling
For happy times and sleepless nights
Toasts for love and a love for healing
Discovered friends and foreign sights
We laughed, we danced, we popped a few
From a distance now remember
Let the youthful warmth return anew
With the sighs of late December
What can we say about four boys
As they grasp the reins of life
A man a woman, God sent joys
A family free of strife
    What matters most and begs no reason
    Our love to you this Christmas season

JMM
1977

CHILDREN`S FEAST

The joy was bórn with an enfant cry
Midst pain and doubt and fears
A Spring of hope welled up through tears
To balm each human sigh

Christmas began as a children`s feast
The moment for innocent dreams
Paths of gold, star filled streams
What seemed to matter most now mattered least

Ah, grasp them close your near and dear
Rejoice their childish ways
Too soon the years lead into days
When we listen but cannot hear

May the Magi`s joy be found anew
Discovered by the child in each of you

JMM
1978

CHRISTMAS SONNET

Existence is a transient joy
Etched fragile by the pen of time
A singular dash of flesh and blood
Lost in the sweep of the mortal line
Harsh falls the verdict on the naïve soul
Obsessed with life`s pace infernal
Unfilled stands crystal designed for wine
Who rejects His vision eternal
Seek out the rainbow that Christmas creates
Through the prism of childhood trust
Warm simple hues based in vivid love
Disguising the gray of timeless dust
  Let the transient joy derive it`s might
  From the soft mellow tones of Christmas night

JMM
1979

CHRISTMAS EVE

Our children have surrendered
Excitement to sleep. And that
Was difficult to leave
When their world cradled a lighted tree

Pine air freshens this city with a plastic
Car wash, that really cleans, across from the green tank
Silent beside the skateboard. How fragile the peace
The night before the day after.

But now tonight
I`ve stopped listening to broken hearts
Or to the fellow on page one killing
To change my mind

It is good I think
To hear Christmas
Each year

And whatever goodwill
Toward men
Was meant to bring

JMM
1983

WHEN THE BOYS COME HOME

December has come by
A year of rushing upon
This night
This night when the boys come home
With dust on their shoes
From a land I onetime knew

Our house now glows from Christmas
Coals within each room—this one
Growing up
That one beyond the door
Growing old
Perhaps slowly
Together we'll explore

Those shadow visions of father and son
Doing their thing alone
Until now
This night
This night

When the boys come home

JMM 1984

LAST PURE CHRISTMAS

It should come as no surprise
Mother
If culled from winter reunions you
Scan the reef and recall our
Last pure Christmas

And when you do recall please reassure
Mother
Tonight when stars are memories
Lighting wave etched portraits
Aged polaroid brown

That we understood even then
Mother
His soft look blessing that final year
Our youngest son saw Christmas
With his heart

JMM
The sea at dusk
Ft Lauderdale Beach
1985

DECISIONS

Tomorrow flowed from innocence
While wishes did come true
As together we dreamed and danced
Around the tree trusting
Young souls on illusions stage

Christmas eve in those days

From when a gentle healing comes
By fifty seasons
To ease regret for choices made
Promises to oneself lost
Beneath the ache of
What might have been

Thankful now I can embrace
With present state of mind
Transformation of past doubt
Even
Grateful that it happened so

Decisions made within the heart
Judged a failure at the time
Perhaps
Perhaps
Though viewed in shadow weigh far less

Than the tragic otherwise
We sometimes bring upon ourselves

JMM 1986

Contemplative Room

"What each must seek in his life never was on land or sea. It is something out of his own unique potentiality for experience, something that never has been and never could have been experienced by anyone else"

Joseph Campbell

"Perhaps the truth depends on a walk around the lake"

Wallace Stevens

MY MOTHER IS A SAINT

I think my mother is a saint

In her whispered miracles, prayer sent
Cures and the B + on my physics test
She meets the cannon`s standards willed
Pontifically by men who preach that men
Know saints and priests know best

There are few models for common types
Praise Kate of Siena, dear Rose of Lima
No Daisy of Dayton nor Bess of Bell Glade
Hermits and virgins, abbots and popes
Johns number twenty to Peter`s sixteen
But this is the stuff from which saints are made

There is no ordinary for ordinary moms
Bathing rude children, forgiving bold men
Martyr to loving her passion for life
She blesses with laughter, counsels with sighs
Makes holy forever
Exemplary days as a dynamite wife

I`ve had my fill of spurious deeds
Bogus relics from spigots at Lourdes
Viewed St Anne`s crutches with prayerful constraint
New nominations list Pious the twelfth
A celibate nurse, a monk of Polish decent—But

I know my mother is a saint

JMM 1998

DIRECTIONS

I have waited for you to ask for directions
Easier to follow than the whispers of preachers
Preaching to change your mind

> Trust Me

Take the first right off the highway
On to the side road then over the rise
Where you will hang a left into the valley

> Trust Me

The road will end suddenly and you must take
The difficult country lane and no other
Lest your life be destroyed

> Trust Me

As you travel look for the signs you missed
The birth of your son a few miles ago
The symphony of orchids explaining
The last crossroad that pointed
To your mother's forgiving smile

> Trust Me

You will see the house across the nameless
River with neither bridge nor skiff to reassure
The decision that must be yours
That will allow Me
To welcome you home

Trust Me

JMM
2013

TURNING 82

Will give cause for some
To believe
That they don`t know
What they are doing
But
Here`s a little secret

Nobody really knows
What the hell they are doing
Nobody

      Suppose if-
      Let`s see
      Over there or
      Maybe here
      So take a shot
      Is he the one or
      Are there two

Parents–presidents-priests
That monk in Tibet
Toss and turn at 2 am
Scrambling to make it up
Thinking

What`s the part of me not thinking
Thinking

JMM 2018

SAPERE AUDE

Breathe the chaos and question
Those questions without answers
That will allow
Thine own self to be true
And perhaps
Change the world

God knows
You might get it right

JMM 2019
Andrew & Olivia
Grandchildren
"dare to know"

GIFT OF LOSS

Earth was not meant to become invisible
Scattered lifeless avenues and squares
Timeless music of time silenced
By demands for distance only to remind
This moment is never again
We are never again

Plagues and wars have always existed
Never rational often surprise
Odious waves of suffering death and
Perhaps
The cruelest evil known
Separation

As matter becomes invisible
We cling to each other
Drifting in clouds sensing
Love is the only anodyne
To moments of anguish
Between life and death

Embrace this gift of loss
Pulsing to unleash
Primordial emotions of care
That will allow
Each morning greeting to soften
Each night's goodbye

JMM
Pandemic 2020

MY FATHER WAS A DOCTOR

In the heart of every true physician
Lies the secret prayer
That years
After he or she is forgotten
Multitudes will be moving
To the measure of their belief and teachings

By living a life dedicated to a sacred tradition
The force of their devotion
The truth of their example
The power of their understanding
The influence of their soul
Will affect eternity

JMM
2020

I do not know the truth, except when it
Becomes part of me
Soren Kierkegaard

MATTER OF FACT

As a matter of fact
You must know
Facts are real not imagined
Never malleable
Easy to measure

Truth requires experience
Deeply captured undefined
Innermost
As a matter of fact
We are here together

Truth is
Infinite love

JMM 2020

*When they heard this sound, a crowd came together
in bewilderment, because each one heard their own
language being spoken.*

Acts 2:4-12

POETRY OF GOD

Deeper longings now direct me
Without need for road maps etched
In Sanskrit or Latin to preach
Thou shalt not today but
Thou shalt do as I say
Tomorrow

Faith declares at birth trusting
Mothers warm embrace beneath
Soft whispers to awaken
Infants from sleep
With their heavenly
Smile

Being in love is never planned when
Sparked emotions appear
Soaring from intimate elated moments
Expressing the inexpressible
In sacred language
Never defined

Grace is delivered to each
Thru culture diverse lyrics
Stories symbols myths providing
Inner thresholds of passage
That will allow the poetry of God
To tell you who you are

JMM
2021

Romance Room

Piglet "How do you spell love?"
Pooh: "You don't spell it you feel it."

- Winnie The Pooh

"Love like crazy!"

- Alvin J. Tight, DDS

COOL NIGHT AIR

Joy to the man with a wife so rare
Who will open the room to the cool night air
My wife`s boudoir mimics King Tut
Once inside, the damn thing stays shut
We discuss at length hygienic criteria
The dangers of dust-eventual ill
But our quiet nights are filled with bacteria
To preserve lasting health, I must take a pill
I`ve tried every trick to improve ventilation
When she is asleep I sneak from the room
How can one survive without inhalation
The air round our bed resembles a tomb
      Give praise to the wife who is willing to please
      By sharing her bed with the soft evening breeze

JMM
1975

KARI

As our lives evolve there is a place
For moistened eyes and deep devotion
Silent smiles, an upturned face
A selfless love of chaste emotion
Our separate trials edge on each day
We hold the bond forever
And as we find a distant way
Our souls are joined together
Thank God for such a blessed time
Men`s lives have very few
In ages hence I`ll sip my wine
Sustained by thoughts of you
      Keep sacred all the joys we shared
      While remembering me as one who cared

JMM
May 4, 1978

EXPLOSIVE LOVE

In time the flame grows cold
The thrill of warmth seems far away
You reach for me-no one to hold
A plea a smile and then dismay
But life still flows as seasons change
The soul continues toward the light
And while the sudden chill is strange
Warm memories sooth the bite
Explosive love yields tense emotion
The nature of the beast
When gone it begs a new devotion
The memory of a feast
     So now rejoice for good times had
     Rather than remember and be sad

JMM
1989

QUIET HOURS

When silence calls the end of day
The frantic world lies still
Soft music balms an anguished will
And sweeps life`s trials away
`Tis then for you my love is clear
Deep knowledge overwhelms my heart
A blessed wife – the vital part
Of all my heart holds dear
The pains of life retard emotion
Submerged in transient things
While quiet hours evoke devotion
To the truth that your love brings
   My love for you derives it`s might
   Within the quiet of the night

JMM
1990

Dana and Pat

Allow me a moment

Falling in love is a good thing but it is not the best thing
Falling in love is a noble feeling, but it is still a feeling
And, no feeling can be relied upon to last in it`s full intensity

Knowledge can last, principles can last but feelings come and go
Feelings are distinct from being, and
Falling in love is distinct from being in love

The being of love is a deep unity, strengthened by habit
Reinforced by a grace
Grace for which both of you must ask
Which does not come easy

Being in love can define your existence
It is not emotion, it is essence
You can be in love even when you do not like each other
Just as you can love yourself even when you do not like yourself

Being in love is the engine on which your marriage will run
Falling in love is only the explosion that starts it
Together from this explosion the essence of your life begins
Trust me, nothing else matters

God speed and God bless

JMM 2006

Adapted from C.S Lewis

Marriage of Dana Panza and Patrick Macdonald

GRAIL CHATEAU

Seductive your silent sermon
Delivered with compassion
Seeds of tested faith
That by your grace now leads
To this Grail Chateau
Our holy place

Rimmed tunnel of French plane trees
Jeweled sunburst in regal pose
Where magic blesses your love to teach
Meaning to garden maze and breeze
Humming whispers in quiet waters
Once deemed out of reach

Bright children dashing past
Mallards drifting diving
All float
Above water and air
Chalk chimneys and turrets
Reflection in the river Cher

Black mourning chambres beyond
Window stretched halls lighting
Historic creations Medici born
Here a sometime answered prayer
There a blueprint
Mercilessly torn

Pray embrace this humble bow
My Queen
For you have promised more
Than dreams may comprehend
The yes to my acceptance
The guide to my sublime
Our Grail Chateau together
Daily
One more time

JMM
Chateau de Chenonceau
France 2007

Dedicated to Kari Macdonald
Composed during a month rental,
vineyard cottage 2 Km from
Chateau de Chenonceau, France

TAO

In French
Sun is always he
Moon is always she
Day is always he
Night is always she
Woman – Man
Harmony of opposites

Yang protects Yin
Yin nurtures Yang
The dance will always remain
Nature's test of balance
When achieved
Everything is one
And the Angels cheer in silence

JMM 2018

THREE WORDS

I felt a crick in my neck
The ache in the back
A reminder of growing years

Bid farewell to a friend
Questioned the news
Searching for hidden truth

Then you were there
Erasing all doubt
In three words that reassured

I love you

JMM
2018

STOLEN POEM FOR KARI

Whenever skies look gray to me and trouble begins to brew
Whenever the winter winds become too strong
I concentrate on you

When fortune cries "Nay, nay" to me
And people declare "You're through"
Whenever the blues become my only songs
I concentrate on you

On your smile, so sweet, so tender
When at first my kiss you do decline
On the light in your eyes when you surrender
And once again our arms intertwine

And so when wise men say to me
That love's young dream never comes true
To prove that even the wise men can be wrong
I concentrate on you

JMM 2021
"I Concentrate on you"

Cole Porter

Haitian Room

"I must remember the things I have seen. I must keep them fresh in memory, see them again in my mind's eye, live through them again and again in my thoughts. And most of all, I must make good use of them in tomorrow's life."

Thomas A Dooley MD

"Participate joyfully in the sorrows of the world. We cannot cure the world of sorrows, but we can choose to live in joy."

Joseph Campbell

GOUTE SEL

The surviving trees lean
With broken arms
Begging
To receive the birds
      That never want to fly here

Above your helpless reef
White by dusty current
Forbidden
To nourish the fish
      That die before they feed here

The moan is Haiti
Over skinned mountains
Where men grow stones thirsting
Beneath your clouds
      That madly refuse to weep here

While your daughter crawls bleeding
This Christmas night
Denied her taste of salt
From a God
      Who never seems to walk here

JMM
Christmas 1987
Port- au- Prince, Haiti

THE PRESS OF MY HAND

There is no noun for this pain
There is no verb for your suffering
There is no prayer for my understanding
As our seconds collide

When now I must share
Without translation
The crush of your despair

The sleeping infant at breast
The gull against the moon
Still moments bursting with silence

Now refuse your never and receive my always
In a transfer of hope
That can only be heard
From the press of my hand

JMM
Medishare Tent Hospital
Post earthquake
Port-au-Prince, Haiti
January 2010

THUNDER

Echo drummed music
Pounding from somewhere below
Trailed by muffled loudspeaker
Preaching

Beyond everyone
Running in place
Rushing to get into heaven
Maybe

The Thunder
I hear from the mountains above
Are sounds from an ancient ceremony
Screaming

To tell them something

JMM
Port-au-Prince, 2018
Nag Hammadi- *The Thunder*

Composed one evening on patio above
Port-au-Prince, hearing church service
preacher and congregation in town below

Some seed fell among thorns, and

the thorns grew up and choked it

(Matt 13:1-9)

MANGOS FOR SALE

She squats on a wicker stool
Back against the red dirt streaked wall
Ignored by silent neighbors
Passing with indifference to prayers
Unanswered for her daily bread

Mangos For Sale

She stares acceptance for this trial of life
Content to carve a way for her children
Captured by the cruel lottery of birth
Culling answers to their questions absent
The harmony of Brahms-the soul of Angelou

Mangos For Sale

Heavy air totes the odor of curbed garbage
Trademark for corruption born poverty
Disorder and banality of violence
Cradle this prison of silent slavery
Woman, you never had a chance

Mangos For Sale

Who will assume guilt
For a nation of smothering thorns
This misplaced abuse of God`s plan
Never will her promise of life flourish
Within the passions of wisdom

Mangos For Sale

JMM 2018, Christ Roi, Haiti

Troubles Room

"It was the best of times, it was the worst of times, it was the age of wisdom, it was the age of foolishness, it was the epoch of belief, it was the epoch of incredulity, it was the season of Light, it was the season of Darkness, it was the spring of hope, it was the winter of despair."

Charles Dickens

"Madness is rare in individuals, but in groups, parties, nations and ages is it the rule."

— Friedrich Nietzsche

PRODIGAL SON

A stalking fog slithers
Under the doors of our ancient home
Snuffing candles designed to glow
Smothering lilacs gasping to grow
The rock on which our lives are anchored
Crumbles to dust from Peter`s stone

Georgie Porgie, pudding and pie,
Kissed the girls and made them cry

We have left the door unlocked
For sacred weapons in hands of twisted minds
Preaching tightrope as path to joy
Defining sex as a guilt stained toy
In silk and satin the Cardinals come and go
Furtively groping Michael Angelo

Mathew, Mark, Luke and John
Bless the bed that I lay on

Sermons preached in psychic bifurcation
From unnatural law dividing Eros and sex
Trashing the magic of human love
In magisterium tomes culled from above
Under the patristic view of the marital text
Defiled as dogma for repeat procreation

There was a crooked man, and he walked a crooked mile.
He found a crooked sixpence upon a crooked stile

Celibacy can provide a saintly life
If achieved by freedom of choice
Required as pretense it serves as mockery
To a preordained life of cleric hypocrisy
Rather- woman – man, yin – yang, plus - minus
Havoc prevented in the oneness of voice

> *I do not like thee, Doctor Fell,*
> *The reason why – I cannot tell*

"But whoso shall offend these little ones
Which believe in me" - has been answered
By cloistered power launching
Vile loathsome criminal suffering
Exposing truth mournfully brought home
Christ died for the sins of Rome

> *A wise old owl lived in an oak*
> *The more he saw the less he spoke*

Denial pervades this dishonest time
Placing blame on society and gays
Accepting penance in fasting terms
Fearing renewal for the Diet of Worms
They moved stained pulpits to rooms realigned
Assuming the guardians of children were blind

> *Diddle, diddle, dumpling, my son John,*
> *Went to bed with his trousers on*

Loneliness weights a millstone on the celibate day
Dependent on brotherzoned friendship to share
The Divine Office, penance and prayer
Cold proxy for the intimacy of marriage
Providing sexual abuse it`s might
In the shadow desert of the rectory night

> *Now I lay me down to sleep,*
> *I pray the Lord my soul to keep*

Salvation depends on a leap of faith
A private pledge to be empty for God
Our need for the meddling cleric is done
They have left us and now we must prod
Them to assume their mundane housekeeping base
While we pray for their return as a prodigal son

> *Humpty Dumpty sat on a wall,*
> *Humpty Dumpty had a great fall.*
> *All the king's horses and all the king's men*
> *Couldn't put Humpty together again*

JMM
August 2018

CONTAGION 2020

Our streets are filled with no ones
That care not who you are
Or how you may have lived
Among political lepers absent
The ability to feel your pain
Without a hand to offer or
Soul to understand

Such creatures do not breed
Rather grow like mold
Feeding off identity guilt and inner decay
Contagion spreading moral ambivalence
Dragging you into beliefs you do not believe
Lest you be labeled unbeliever
A grim level of unclean

All lies matter
Coerced by spurious questions
Providing heard immunity
For academic elites in safe rooms
Deaf to historical moans of dying nations
Denied consensus healing for
The common good

How painfully alien the world can seem
Unmoved by reason or logic
Compelled to kneel in disrespect
For those who died to earn respect
Equating justice with violent revenge
Compassion with resentment defining
Political correctness

Contagions fear the immune response
Derived from faith instilled value
Creating lethal defense that annuls
Antigens of prejudice and hate
Brothers and sisters are dying
America is burning
And the band plays on

JMM 2020
American political turmoil

OUR SUPERVISOR

Our parent, which art somewhere, in equality be thy name
Our native conquered land come, the will of the electorate sometimes
be done
By media driven acclimation as is its nature
And as it damn well should be around here.
Give us this day our deserved bread
And forgive my friend`s felonies as we forgive criminals who are only
human against us
And lead us not by political propaganda
But deliver us from the other conniving party, be it Blue or Red
For this is our space, the subterfuge and the unearned spoils
For ever and ever
At least until the next election

Amen / Awoman-

                                        Ode to Progressive Secularism-2021

Heritage Room

Ruth Johnson Macdonald--Poet

"We are not human beings having a spiritual experience. We are spiritual beings having a human experience."

Pierre Teilhard de Chardin

"To live a superficial life is to do damage to your soul."

Thomas Merton

WHAT IS HEAVEN LIKE

What is heaven like
I wonder
Breathless beauty
Startling
As thunder

Joys that transcend
All
I`ve ever known
Love immeasurable
Still unborn

All of this
And
Yet I hope
Heaven
Is a quiet place

Down beside the sea
Where I can talk
To God
And He
Can talk to me

RJM- Brigantine, N.J

IDLE SUFFERING

Idle suffering
Is not ordained
And can wisely be
Profaned

For joy can be
A saintly habit
As pleasing to God
As a long fasting Abbot

RJM
Mepkin Abby, SC

MOTHER`S DREAMS

Who will walk this garden after me
And in what distant day
Behold the blossoms
White upon the branches
Caressing every tree

Who will open wide
My kitchen door
And scatter crumbs
To feed
A thousand birds or more

What other wife will stand one day
And feel the gentile fragrance
Rise from a Spring filled land
And dream such dreams
As only mothers can

For her who waits here
In the stillness of an April night
To whatever stranger
Makes this place her own
I bequeath the tender joy
Of each new morning`s trembling light
      And all the love for everything of God`s
      My hungry soul has known

RJM- Hilton Head, NC

SOMETIMES BE YOUR MARY

Let me
Sometimes be your Mary
At your feet
Content with love
This vigil Jealously
I will keep

Or still must I be your Martha
Busily burdened by things ever
Forever
Serving
When my thoughts
Are soaring on wings

But hungry and needy
Are many
That seek my willing hands
To comfort
Feed and cloths them
Are these then your demands

Will you fill me
With moments of quiet
To listen in the silence of the night
To hear when there is no music
To ride
With the stars in their flight

So that out of my clutter
I will find you
As part of each busy day
To still be a serving Martha
      Yet with Mary`s spirit to pray

RJM

HUMILITY`S SIDE

I try for each virtue
In opposition to pride
And strive unassuming
To be on humility`s side

But just when I think
I have conquered my ego
At that very moment
I have no longer a halo

RJM

LET IRELAND BE MY SHELTER

When I must cry
Let Ireland be my shelter
Even under her weeping sky

When I dare to laugh
Let her song
Of ringing bells
That break with joy
Across quiet morning air
Across meadows green
Find an echo there
That I can share

Let her flowing streams
Beneath the fields of purple heather
Be my peace

So that never will the joy
Of her within me
Ever
Ever cease

RJM-Ballyvaughan, Ireland

LET MINE BE JOY

Of all the gifts
Of the Holy Spirit
Let mine be joy
And let the whole world
Hear it

For joy
Has the quality
Priceless and rare
That can mix with
To soften
Each troublesome care

RJM

TREASURED GIFTS

There is no legacy
No world of wealth
To give you

But only treasured gifts
As these
For you to take

My simple faith
To guide you
Through unknown seas
Or narrow sandy shoals
To quiet harbors

My joy to see
A cardinal in the snow
A willow in the wind
To hear a robin's song
In April

My childhood courage
To stand and face
Whatever sorrow or defeat
Comes suddenly
Across your way

My inspiration
To awaken
Whatever greatness
Lies sleeping
In your soul

And most of all

My love
Down through
All these years
That bound your wounds
And dried
Your baby tears

RJM -164 Vernon Drive
Pittsburgh, Pa

I AM ONE

I am part of everything
That grows
From every star
That`s hung across
The velvet sky

I am part of every cloud
The westwind blows
In quiet morning light
Or in the depth and
Solitude of night

I am one with every heart
That cries in lonely fear
And joyous
Am I with those
Who shout for all to hear

I am part of very prayer
Of hope
That reaches
Up to grasp
God`s hand

And I am one
With all the love
That forever pours out
On a trembling broken land.

RJM 1945

FIRST STRING

Little boy
Grown tall and strong
You come
With tear stained face
And child heart newly broken
Bewildered by your first defeat

My mother's soul
Within me
Is filled with sorrow
Looking up to see you
Standing head bowed
Forlornly in the doorway
And my arms
In tenderness go out
To shield you
From this thing
That has laid it's hurting hand
On your young years

In haste
I send a silent prayer
To storm the heavens
For the word to bring you
Blessed comfort
To let you lift your boyish head
And smile again
And face your young friends
So quick to ridicule

Oh can`t you see
Dear yielded part of me
There is more nobility
In losing gracefully
And who will know or care
A hundred years from now
Whether or not you made
　　　`First String`

RJM
1948

SAVE YOUR SORROW

Let there be none
With tears to shed
Nor mourn for me
When I am dead

For what a waste
Such things would be
When I`m content
In eternity

Save your sorrow
And soul filled weeping
For a world gone mad
With its evil keeping

Be glad for me
Rejoice with singing
My life`s merely changed
And just beginning

RJM

ABOUT AUTHORS

Ruth Johnson Macdonald-RJM (1913-2013) was born in Pittsburgh, Pennsylvania. She received her education at St Genevie's Academy, Ashville North Carolina and Mary Washington College, Fredrickson Virginia. She was the devoted wife of RR Macdonald MD, Pediatrician, Pittsburgh, Pennsylvania and the mother of John Macdonald MD, the eldest of their six children. Ruth Macdonald was a remarkable visionary. Through her painting, artistry and transcendent based poetry, her legacy defines the essence of Cultural Heritage.

John M Macdonald, MD, FACS, is a native of Pittsburgh, Pennsylvania. He received a Bachelor of Science degree at the University of Notre Dame and his Medical Degree at the University of Pennsylvania, School of Medicine. Internship served at Jackson Memorial Hospital, University of Miami. Military duty as Captain in the United States Air Force. Residency in general and thoracic surgery at the University of Pittsburgh Medical Center. Fellowship in thoracic and cardiovascular surgery as Senior Registrar, St Bartholomew's Hospital, London England.

Dr. Macdonald is Board Certified in general surgery and thoracic surgery. From 1971 until 1999, he practiced thoracic and vascular surgery in Ft Lauderdale, Florida. Dr. Macdonald was the Chief of Surgery, Holy Cross Hospital, Ft. Lauderdale, Florida from 1988-1991. Over the past 25 years, Dr. Macdonald has been extensively involved in the clinical and research aspects of wound care and lymphedema. He has lectured extensively both in North America and internationally. Dr. Macdonald has authored numerous articles and text chapters relating to both lymphedema and wound related lymph stasis. In 2002 he was appointed to the faculty of the Department of Dermatology and Cutaneous Surgery at the University of Miami, Miller School of Medicine. In May 2014, at the Spring meeting of the Society for the Advancement of Wound Care, Dr. Macdonald received the 14th annual John Boswick Award for "Outstanding Lifetime Achievement in Wound Healing".

In the first two days, post- earthquake, January 12, 2010, Dr. Macdonald established the wound care program in the University of Miami, Project Medishare, Haitian Relief Tent Hospital in Port-au-Prince. He served as Medical Director of this program, now located at Hospital Bernard Mevs in Port-au-Prince, Haiti, from 2011 until January 2021.